LET'S TALK ABOUT

BEING SELFISH

REVISED FOR EDUCATIONAL USE

By Joy Wilt Berry

Illustrated by John Costanza

CHILDRENS PRESS, CHICAGO

Let's talk about BEING SELFISH. 3

Have you ever been with people
who would not
share their food with you?

5

Have you ever played with people
who would not
share their toys with you?

People who do not share
are SELFISH.

They care more about themselves
than about others.

9

When you are with someone
who is selfish,
    how do you feel?
    what do you think?
    what do you do?

When you are with someone
who is selfish,
you may feel
left out and angry.

You may not want
to be with that person.

13

It is important to treat others
the way you want to be treated.

If you want others
to share with you,
you will have
to share with them.

You will have to be unselfish.

15

Being unselfish
does not mean
you have to share
all your things
all the time.

Sometimes you can't share.

17

If you do not have
enough food to share,
just put the food away.

Try not to eat
in front of anyone
who does not have
anything to eat.

19

If you are going to share,
try to be fair.

Here is a good rule for sharing:
    Let one person divide.
    Let the other one choose.

If you have something special,
you may not want to share it.

Try not to use it
in front of another person
unless
    the other person
    does not want to use it, or
    the other person
    has something else to use.

You do not have to share
with anyone who is careless.

Put your things away
if you think
they may be lost or damaged.

25

When you share,
it sometimes helps to show
how things work,
and how they
should be cared for.

27

When one thing
must be shared by two,
be fair.

Take turns.

Let each person use it
for the same amount of time.

It helps to use
a clock or a timer.

29

To be happy, treat others
the way you want to be treated.

Everyone is happier
when no one acts selfish.